WINGS OF WHITE

WINGS OF WHITE

MARJORIE WHEELER

AuthorHouse™ UK Ltd.
1663 Liberty Drive
Bloomington, IN 47403 USA
www.authorhouse.co.uk
Phone: 0800.197.4150

Published by AuthorHouse 01/22/2014

ISBN: 978-1-4918-8658-8 (sc)
ISBN: 978-1-4918-8662-5 (e)

About Marjorie's Book

<u>Just Between us Lord</u> - As the title of this first section implies, these poems do have an intimate and prayerful tone, I hope, dear readers that you will find words here that will lead you to quiet prayer.

<u>Imagine (Picture Poems)</u> - Imagination is a wonderful gift from God. To be able to see in the mind's eye as you read the words, bringing them to life. The more we use this lovely gift, the more we appreciate the work of God's hands.

<u>Praise</u> - How naturally this section follows on from the previous one. These hymn-like poems are written with the hope that the words will sing in both the joyful and saddened heart.

<u>For the Little Ones</u> - These are picture poems written for the little ones, in the hope that they might excite their lively imaginations and encourage them to draw, colour or write about them, just as they see them.

<u>A Taste of Christmas</u> - Sometimes just a little taste of something can make us want to repeat it again and again. These few poems are my 'Taste of Christmas' just for you.

<u>The Shy Little Star</u> - This story is especially for our young ones. Maybe the Title 'The Shy Little Star' will encourage the shy ones to discover how even 'they' can do something wonderful.

<u>Marjorie's Snippets</u> - I suppose that thinking aloud might be a good way to describe these varied poems. They speak of ordinary day to day happenings, but have a wee 'twist in the tail'. Maybe bringing a wry smile or nod or two.

<u>Quiet Meditations</u> - There is deep meaning in these words, please do not rush through them, rather read slowly, just as though sucking a delightful sweet.

"This is my work for you, in His Name."

Appreciation

I would like to give my grateful thanks to all who have
encouraged and helped me to move ahead with this new book-
'Wings of White'
I particularly want to give sincere thanks and appreciation
for all the careful work entailed, by my artistic friend
Mrs Mary Page
who designed the cover.
Marjorie

Dedication

I quietly dedicate this book
to the memory of my niece,
Marion Christine Cross
Who not only bravely coped
with terminal cancer, but
during her illness, wrote a book
to help others in a similar situation
entitled "Living With Terminal Cancer."

Contents

Just between us Lord

IMAGINE (PICTURE POEMS)

PRAISE

FOR THE LITTLE ONES

A TASTE OF CHRISTMAS

THE SHY LITTLE STAR

MARJORIE'S SNIPPETS

QUIET MEDITATIONS

Just between us Lord

A Garden In My Heart

I have a garden in my heart
Where Jesus walks each day.
I know the way to ask Him in,
I simply have to pray.

I have a garden in my heart
Which flowers all year round.
There's Peace among the blossoms
Where Jesus can be found.

The flowers in my heart are sweet,
Where walks my precious Lord;
Refreshed by Love unspeakable,
Fed by His Living Word.

There's a garden up in heaven,
Where God's bright angels sing
With voice too pure for human ears,
They glorify our King.
They glorify our King!

Come By Faith

Let us come, but not in haste,
Draw near to Thee as in holy place.
Let us come, our souls be calm,
The Love and Peace of God our balm.

Let us come with silent awe,
And humbly bow our heads in prayer.
Come by faith in Christ our Lord,
The Son of God, the Living Word.

Rise up now, the day awaits;
Come gird yourselves with armour holy.
Guarded from the evil foe,
Strong in the Name of Christ we go.

"Come Gently Now"

Come gently now, our Father waits
To meet His child in prayer.
Turn from the throbbing drums of life,
His tranquil Peace to share.

Come softly now, with humble joy,
As spirit drawn toward Thine
Awaits with patient, open soul
Your Will, O Love Divine.

Go bravely now, the tryst is o'er,
Assured He holds us dear.
In silence has He touched the soul,
We have no cause to fear!

Comfort

When heartache sharply pierces
The depths none else can know;
When rainbows disappear from view,
And streams of tears o'erflow.

When memory, keener than a blade
Cuts through the mind unbidden,
Revealing pictures of the past,
Of sharing times long hidden.

Think then of love received and given,
For love endures for ever.
Though tender now this cord that binds,
No-one, no, none can sever.

This is the pattern of our pain,
The anguish of our grief;
A measure of our life-long love,
May this truth bring deep relief.

Fit For Purpose

Here is my heart, Lord Jesus,
Here is my heart for You.
It beats only for You Lord,
Oh, keep it ever true.

Here is my soul, Lord Jesus
I raise it Lord to You.
Make it 'fit for purpose' Lord,
Thus blessing all I do.

Here is my life, Lord Jesus,
I bring it Lord with prayer.
Take and use it as You will,
Your Love, Your Joy to share.

Here is my song, Lord Jesus,
My song of love for You.
Oh, may I sing Your praises
Till earthly life is through.

Friend above all friends

Friend above all friends,
Help me be a friend like You.
Never waning, ever bright,
Others first in all I do.

O Friend who never fails us,
Keep me steadfast, keep me true.
Be it day, or be it night,
Bringing everything to You.

O Friend, that Day is coming
When prayers will all be known.
May those whose hearts we pray for
Rejoice as You call them HOME.

Have I lost You?

Have I lost You, Christ my Saviour
Amidst the stress of pain and woe?
Vainly grasping earthly comforts
Ashamed my Lord, for doing so.

Guiltily I try to pray Lord,
Like a child with inner fear.
Reaching out for hands to comfort,
Simply hoping You may hear.

Could this be Your 'way of healing'
First the dragon, then the dove?
Your Spirit guiding me to find Lord,
Words of Cleansing, words of Love.

You have found me—Christ my Saviour!
Foolishly I went astray;
Now those nail-pierced hands will comfort
As I praise You, as I pray.

He sees our tears

He sees our tears even before we cry,
He hears our groans even before they are made.

In the deep, deep night we call to You,
Alone in the darkness.
But, we are not alone,
We are not alone.

As the sunrise opens the curtains of the night,
So too, Your presence brings to our souls Your Light.
The answer to prayer in blessings shown.

Our Wonderful God! Our Wonderful God!
We should have known—

You see our tears—even BEFORE we cry!

I need You Lord

I need You Lord, each dawning day,
So often cannot find the way,
What to think, to do, to say;
Quite simply Lord—I need You.

I need You Lord, when hours are long,
Feeling alone amidst the throng.
Voices speak, I hardly hear, because
Dear Lord—I need You.

I need You Lord, in darkest night,
When clouds of sorrow hide Your Light.
Then I struggle hard to pray
This heartfelt phrase—I need You.

I need You Lord, as time flows on,
Tomorrow comes, today has gone.
As faith returns, strength grows anew.
You always know, dear Lord,
You always know—I need You!

I shall not fear

O gracious Holy Spirit,
Thank You for bringing me to God's Word.
I humbly pray You will help my mind
And heart, to absorb and remember His Truths.
Growing ever stronger in faith,
And walking with a trusting heart,
Through the unknowns of each tomorrow.

Thus, with the Lord's Promise to 'always be with me,'
I shall not fear.
Believing in my heart that You, dear Lord,
Will stay for ever near.

"All praise be to God!"

I wish Lord

I WISH I could write from the heart Lord,
With words that could speak' soul to soul.'
To know Your Love and Your tender care,
Making the broken-hearted whole.

I WISH I could act with Your Love Lord,
Reaching out as from 'friend to friend',
Bringing Peace and Calm to a troubled mind,
Showing Your Love has no end.

I WISH I could pray as You taught Lord,
On that hill above Galillee.
Feeling the power of Your Spirit's flow,
Even to one such as me.

I WISH I could walk in Your Way Lord,
Though the pathway be steep and long;
Knowing Your hand guides my every step,
My heart should burst forth with song.

Jesus, take me by the hand

Jesus, take me by the hand,
Your unseen hand hold mine.
In Yours this trembling hand is strong,
O Precious Love Divine.

Jesus, take me by the hand,
As Shepherd calm my fears.
How tenderly You lift me high
And wipe away my tears.

Jesus, take me by the hand,
O Living Promise True.
All trembling gone, my soul set free,
Until You take me home with You.

Lead Thou us on

Lead Thou us on we humbly pray,
Lead Thou us on from day to day.
In love those early seeds were sown,
Today, we claim Christ as our own.

Jesus, You are our Holy Friend,
From when we wake to each day's end.
"I'm always near," Your Promise True,
Help us each day our faith renew.

Teach us dear Lord, to share with You
Each step we take, and all we do.
To seek Your help in what we've planned,
To know and trust You understand.

Lead Thou us on in twilight hour,
Safe and secure within Thy power.
To wait in peace the trumpet tone,
When Christ in glory, claims His own.

The Mirror

Lord, I have been looking,
And I shall look again.
I was looking in a mirror,
A mirror blurred by pain.

Overwhelmed, I quite forgot
Just where I should begin;
Instead of looking up, my Lord,
I was looking in.

Battles fought within my mind,
Just fed a deepening fear.
Shadows swiftly darken Lord,
When we forget You're near.

Through a cloudy mirror Lord,
My human eyes see Thee.
Then Lord, Your Spirit tells me this—
HOW CLEARLY YOU SEE ME!

The Mountain

In the quiet of the night
I meet with You, my Lord;
Silence here is palpable,
Beating with my heart.

No distractions in this hour,
A holy time, my Lord.
When Spirit calls to spirit—
Love alone the language.

The sleeping world knows nothing,
A sacred tryst, my Lord;
Unheard music fills my soul,
Each note a prayer to God.

The light of day is breaking,
Time to descend, my Lord.
To take again the strain of life,
While heart and soul—remember!

Our love for Him is flowing

Our love for Him is flowing,
As humbly we draw near;
The Peace of Jesus in our hearts
So precious and so dear.

The Love of Jesus dying,
We bow our heads in shame.
We ask forgiveness here and now,
Just trusting in His Name.

The joy of sins forgiven,
Our covenant with God.
Redemption, Peace, eternal Hope,
Through Jesus Christ our Lord.

Then let us raise our voices
To reach our Father's throne.
Let love and thanks pour freely forth,
Most surely, we're His own!

Our Privilege

No heart can hold the bounty of Your Love Lord,
Rushing in as full as mountain stream.
My heart would surely burst wide open Lord,
Were I to try to hold it close within.

Oh, open wide the floodgates of my heart Lord,
Let nothing bar or stem love's onward flow.
As rays of sunshine melt the frozen fields Lord,
May others find in me—Your inner glow.

No deed can fully bless another heart Lord,
Unless we hold each little act in prayer.
The finest deed without Your Love is worthless,
Our privilege to bring Your Love and share.

Peace of Jesus

Peace of Jesus, fall upon us
As we meet You here in prayer.
We would bring the needs of others,
Bring them in our love and care.

Father, spread Your wings around them,
Meet their deepest needs each day
With comfort, healing, hope and courage,
This, in Jesus' Name we pray.

Joy of spirit Lord You give us,
As we slowly walk away.
We have humbly brought before You
Dear and needing ones today.

So, with grateful hearts we leave them
Safely in our Father's care.
In His wisdom He will answer
Each and every heart-felt prayer.

Peace—Joy—Love

The PEACE we know when we draw near to You
Is but a glimpse of the PEACE OF HEAVEN.

The JOY we know when aware You are near
Is but a glimpse of the JOY OF HEAVEN.

The LOVE we know as we worship You
Is but a glimpse of the LOVE OF HEAVEN.

For these we thank You, Lord our God,
For these we praise Your Holy Name!

Praying for Another

When a friend prays for another friend in Jesus,
Most surely, both are blessed.

When one prays with a forgiving heart for the one who hurts them,
Most surely, it can open a door for our Lord to reach out and
Begin to soften the unkind heart.

When a friend who prays is caring and sharing the pain of another,
Most surely, the suffering one shall be comforted.

When a friend prays faithfully for a friend of 'faith' whose life is ebbing
away,
Most surely, our Lord will come close, take their hand, and will—
LIGHT THEIR WAY HOME!

A Rainbow Prayer

How hard it is sometimes to pray
For someone close at heart.
Somehow the words we feel inside,
Dry up before we start.

It's not because we do not care,
The opposite more true.
There seems so much we want to ask
In love, dear friend for you.

How well we know, how oft we're told
There's One who understands.
We bring you, dear one before Him now,
And trust His caring hands.

And so, dear one, we pray for you,
Our hearts ache for your pain.
But love will keep us very near
Until we meet again.

The Promise that each rainbow brings
Remains for ever true.
Without the darkness in our life—
How can Love's Light shine through!

Remembrance

The air recoiled from thunderous blast,
From weapons built to kill, destroy.
The cries for help are silent now,
Erupting earth as velvet lawn.

Head high, steps strong, the unseen heroes march,
Step out in spirit at the bugle call.
Today's brave heroes, following their lead,
Comrades together, one in destiny.

"Take up your cross and follow Me!"
Christ's battle cry today.
Remembrance strikes the heart with pride,
And blessed throngs respond.

Our way is plain, His calling clear,
To honour them our duty.
Through wars and schisms, and nature wild,
Until Christ comes in VICTORY!

Serenity

In the Peace that You give us,
Our souls find rest.

In the Love that You bring us,
Our hearts are blest.

Your calm and serenity
Surround us here.

As safe in Your Presence,
We know no fear.

As the Grace of Your Spirit
Calls to our soul.

In Sacred Communion,
Our hearts are made whole.

Silent Waiting

O gentle Peace
Come fill our hearts,
O Dove of heaven descend.
O Breath of Calm
Serene and pure,
Our breath with Thine we blend.

O Gracious One
In silence now,
We seek Your Precious Word.
O Holy Spirit
Safe in Your care,
By evil undisturbed.

Sorrow into Joy

I weep inside and love You Lord,
Where no-one else may see.
My Lord, Your Living Word reveals
How much Your Love for me.

I weep inside and ponder Lord,
On those who live in fear;
Oh, may Your Word assurance bring,
That Christ Himself draws near.

I weep inside and bring my sins,
My head bent low in shame.
What Mercy, Grace and Pardon Lord,
For one who caused Your pain.

I sing aloud with joy, my Lord,
My Risen Saviour LIVES!
As echoes strongly o'er the years,
"This Son of God—FORGIVES!"

Speak to me Lord

Speak to me Lord, with voice so low and kind,
Comfort and soothe the worries of my mind;
When in distress Thy people cried to Thee,
Like them, I call Lord, "Do Thou come to me."

Speak to me Lord, as to an erring friend,
Look down with Love as I before Thee bend;
When full of sin, Thy people cried to Thee,
Like them, I call Lord, "Do Thou come to me."

Speak to me Lord, tell me of joys to come,
Let mercy flow through Jesus Christ Your Son;
When round Thy throne, Thy face Your dear ones see,
Call me, like them dear Lord, to come to Thee.

Until That Day

When Christians part, the ties remain secure;
Bound in the Love of Jesus Christ our Lord.
So, as we part, our love stays with you all.
God's Peace and Joy be yours for evermore.

Remember then each dear one with a smile,
The times we've shared His Peace and Joy and Love.
And in this Peace our spirits blend as one;
Until 'That Day' when we shall meet above.

Wait on the Lord

Wait on, wait on, wait on the Lord,
The battle has begun.
'tis time to heed our Captain's call,
Be faithful to God's Son.

Pray on, pray on, pray to the Lord,
What God has planned shall be.
In Him alone our strength is set,
O blessed Trinity.

Believe, believe with all your heart,
God's Word for ever true.
No evil force may overcome,
Through Christ your power renew.

Let's watch and pray, obey our Lord,
The time is drawing near.
Each faithful soul shall hear His voice—
"FEAR NOT, FOR I AM HERE!"

We Bring Our Hearts

We bring our hearts, Lord Jesus,
We bring our hearts to You.
They beat for You alone Lord,
Oh, keep them ever true.

We bring our song, Lord Jesus,
Our song of love for You.
Oh, may we sing Your praises
Till earthly life is through.

We bring our life, Lord Jesus,
We bring it Lord with prayer,
Oh, use it as You will Lord,
Your Love, Your Joy to share.

We raise our soul to You Lord,
Have mercy Lord today;
As spirit breathes to Spirit,
All glory Yours, we pray.

We come into Your Presence Lord

We come into Your presence Lord,
With hungry soul and humble heart.
We bow before Your presence now:
"Have mercy Lord," we pray, we pray.

The wine is poured, the bread awaits,
Symbols of Your Sacrifice.
We pause to pray before we take;
"Forgive us Lord," we pray, we pray.

"This is my Body—this is my Flesh,
Take eat it, and remember Me.
This is my Blood—shed for your sake;
"Oh cleanse us Lord," we pray, we pray.

The precious hour comes to an end,
Too soon the fractious world draws near.
Again we face temptation's voice;
"Protect us Lord," we pray, we pray.

When in God's time we're called to rest,
When all our earthly struggles cease;
Oh! May we hear Thy blessed call—
"Come to Me child, today, today."

With Silent Awe

Let us come, but not in haste,
Draw near to Thee as in holy place.
Let us come, our souls be calm,
The Love and Peace of God our balm.

Let us come with silent awe,
And humbly bow our heads in prayer.
Come by faith in Christ our Lord,
The Son of God, the Living Word.

Rise up now, the day awaits,
Come gird yourselves with armour holy.
Guarded from the evil foe,
Strong in the Name of Christ, we go!

Your Father Knows

Move ever onward, anxious soul,
Your Lord still leads the way.
When darkest clouds of doubt appear,
His Light brings break of day.

Look ever upward, trusting soul,
Your Home awaits you there.
The climb is hard, the climb is long,
Each step a whispered prayer.

Abide in peace, dear child of God,
Enfolded in His wings.
Take heart when worldly fears arise,
Your Father knows—all things.

Your Still Small Voice

Oh Lord, let Your Peace fall upon this place,
Gently—Gently.

Oh Lord, let Your hand shield us from distraction,
Lovingly—Lovingly.

Oh Lord, let us know Your Spirit's Grace,
Humbly—Humbly.

Oh Lord, we come to meet with You now,
Silently—Silently.

Oh Lord, may we hear within Your 'still small voice',
Softly—softly.

Imagine
(Picture Poems)

Colours

Look at a rainbow where skies are dark,
Look at a bubble or fountain spray.
Look 'neath a waterfall thundering down,
Or morning sky at dawn of the day.

Look at the patchwork nature has wrought,
Look how the threads of a tapestry blend.
Look at an infant's first effort at art,
Or evening sky at summer day's end.

Colours surround us, within, without;
Red glowing faces, blue frozen hands.
Emerald green of a covetous eye,
Faces of people from far away lands.

So hard to select one perfect tone,
So hard to choose a favourite hue;
The silver of youth, the golden of age,
God's heaven my choice, it has to be BLUE!

Gala Day in Aberaeron

The sun is warm as voices murmer,
They sing a descant to the sea;
On full parade the boats stand silent,
Keels await the tide's returning,
To know again the pulse of surging
And cross again the bar with me.

The sudden piercing scream of the gulls,
Who sense the banquet flowing in;
As crabs find shelter 'neath deep water,
Safe from the jam jar and the pin.
Like the paddling feet of stately swans
The keels move smoothly 'neath the hulls.

The tide is full, there's a gentle swell,
A spectacular armarda;
The sails are set fine, the wind blows strong,
The eager rigging sings for joy'
Full primed each vessel awaits the gun.
Time for courage, strength and drama.

Prow as sharp as arrow in full flight
Set by the Skipper's skilful hand;
Instantly his crew obey each call,
As swirling foam tells of their speed.
First around the buoy they safely fly;
To boom and cheers the winners land.

All is quiet now, the boats are still,
They lie at rest by moonlight glow.
A familiar figure stops awhile,
The Skipper on his homeward way.
They share the secrets of running wave,
That only she and he may know.

The Hazel Tree

How versatile the hazel tree,
With branches straight and true.
Her dainty leaves in early Spring,
Sprout forth in greenest hue.

But wait, what's this we can espy
A-fluttering in the breeze?
Why! Dancing brightly o'er our heads
Bright golden lamb's tails please.

Young sparrow, finch or tiny wren
Feel safe in hazel nest;
Tucked snugly down in leafy bow'r,
Their tiny babies rest.

With Autumn skies and chilly winds,
Her giving still not done;
She offers nut-brown clusters sweet,
Enough for everyone.

A hedgerow friend the hazel tree,
For squirrel furry red.
In cosy nook, all curled up tight,
Shy dormouse safe in bed.

Helping Hands

The passing winds blow hot, blow cold,
Put out my hands, no bars to hold.
Harsh storms of life draw ever near;
I hide my face—no shelter here.

A shrunken world, house-high, house-long,
Of netted eyes, of muffled song.
Like madd'ning midges in the sky,
A myriad questions asking, "Why? "Why?"

Doors abound of every kind,
No keys, no locks, they're of the mind.
As human figures, huddled low
Go scuttling by—how can they know!

Then suddenly, a ray of light;
They come and make a dark day bright.
A nod, a smile, a helping hand,
These are the friends who UNDERSTAND.

The Hungry Ones

How beautiful our world appears,
Serene, secure and sweet.
What calm surrounds our Homeland,
Where sea and mountain meet.
What bounty rich our larder fills,
With fruits of earth and sea.
While beasts of farm in plenty,
Grow strong for you and me.

But stop a moment, think awhile
Of other lands afar.
Where earth is barren, wasted,
By famine and by war.
How hard for us to comprehend
The pain that meets our eyes;
A mother, gaunt and helpless,
As her baby slowly dies.

While half our world has ample food,
The rest know deepest need;
While half the world is caring,
The rest know only greed.
How urgent is the message now,
To follow Christ's own lead.
A time for selfless giving,
The hungry ones to feed.

To pray is not enough alone,
We need to act today;
Giving freely of ourselves,
To wipe their tears away.

Imagine

Imagine yourself as the morning sun
Peeps so shyly over the hill.
The proud cockerel crowing to greet the dawn,
While all else is secret and still.

Imagine yourself as the noon-day sun
Burns brazen and bright in the sky.
How welcome, how cool the shade of the trees,
That sweeten the breeze wafting by.

Imagine yourself in the twilight hour,
That piercing and glorious light.
Blushing pink clouds hover over your head,
Every colour startlingly bright.

Imagine yourself as darkness seeps
From the East toward the West.
The moon, in diamond-studded sky
As God lights His children's rest.

Imagine yourself with time standing still,
No more the bright stars above;
As light indescribable floods the world,
Being caught in His arms of Love.

Kindness

'Kindness', what a simple word, like touch, or smile or tear.
Yet, none can purchase kindness, indeed the cost would be too dear.

It seems to me, that many folk make up an unseen chain;
Where links are forged by suffering, by anguish, heartache, pain.

I had never thought of kindness as something one could read;
Your Book Lord, shows there is a way to share our neighbour's need.

It's like a visit from a friend, a friend who understands,
For, as I read, I'm comforted, wrapt in those loving unseen hands.

Oh Lord, true kindness comes from You, now show us how to share
Your comfort, and your tenderness, in Jesus Name to love and care.

Letters

This morning a letter popped in through my door,
The writing I knew, I had seen it before.
With great joy I opened it, could scarcely wait,
While my first cup of tea grew cold in the grate.

Isn't it lovely, the thrill we discover
As we read on from one page to another;
For somehow to me it's like meeting a friend.
I'm always quite sad when I come to the end.

Of course we enjoy having chats on the phone,
But that's little comfort when feeling alone.
I'm happy to browse, be it scrawling or neat,
Enjoying each line, just like sucking a sweet.

So, when I reply to your letter my friend,
You too, might be sad when you come to the end.
It goes without saying—friends understand
How a letter from you feels like 'holding your hand'.

Light of Love, of Joy, of Peace

Light to guide our wandering way,
Light as darkness turns to day.
Light that shines within a dream,
Or healing light from laser beam.

Light of Love, of Joy, of Peace,
Light of God, never to cease.
Light where deeds of darkness done,
Bright Light which makes those demons run.

Light that opens new-born eyes,
Light to earth from distant skies.
Light that comforts in death's hour,
Eternal Light of heavenly power.

"I am the Light," our Saviour tells;
No darkness where His Spirit dwells.
Hold fast this Truth, oh anxious heart,
God loves His own, He'll ne'er depart.

Melody

I had a glimpse of heaven today,
Shown to me by my Lord.
With inner joy I sensed His call,
He drew me to His Word.

I felt God's blessings reaching me,
My heart warmed to His touch.
I bowed my head as prayer flowed free—
"I love You God, so much!"

His Spirit blessed me with a song,
Rainbow pure, so fleeting.
Heaven's harmony that touched my soul,
Our 'Melody of Meeting'.

Moving Day

What a muddle!
What a mess!
Chaos everywhere today.
Boxes, bundles,
Yards of string,
Because we're moving far away.

"Where's the scissors?
Where's the tape?
Will someone help me move this please?"
Dust is flying,
Spiders run—
"A-ah! tissues quick, I'm going to sneeze!"

I'm not ready!
Here's the van!
Surely, nothing could be worse than this.
In they come,
The moving men.
"Relax now, we'll soon sort you Miss".

Turn the key,
It's time to go.
Another page of history waits;
Excitement grows,
Nearly there—
'It's 'Welcome Home', through open gate.

Music of Life

The senses God has given us
Can bring a message pure.
To smell the sea, to see the clouds,
Or touch the fragile flower.
We give Him thanks for all He shares
With us His own, His kin.
Surely, music's pleasures rare
Can only come from Him.

The jazzman loves his trumpet,
Soft glides the cellist's bow.
Throbbing drums and tympani
Why, e'en the deaf may know.
Silent monks toll solemn gong,
Bright pagodas tinkling bells;
Within us all, as fancy leads,
Life's music gently swells.

Those who have no gift to use
To play, to dance, to sing,
May seek the joy of nature's sounds,
Like rustling grasses bring.
Contented anglers gladly tell
Of plopping fish that play.
Shifting pebbles on the shore,
As sundown ends the day.

God compensates the loss of sense,
Of feeling, touch and sound;
When one lessens so it seems
A deeper sense is found.
For feelings deep within our hearts
Are beautiful and rare;
None can surely be as rich
As music, sprung from prayer!

Rain Power

Pools of water, tranquil, calm;
Do not disturb their silence.
Whispering wavelets on the shore,
Kissing infant toes so gently.

Sparkling streamlets laugh and bubble,
As paddling children squeal with joy.
Broad rivers glide with stately grace,
Yet, deadly currents hide below.

United now with surging power,
Tamed by man for mankind's need.
Consider how it all began,
Life-giving raindrops by God's hand.

Bound together with one purpose,
We too, like raindrops gather force.
Love from heaven, or hate from hell?
The choice is stark, no middle way—
The Call goes out—"Come, choose today!"

The Owls at Sundown

The changing light alerts her,
An urgent instinct to hunt awakens.
With one last look, she leaves them
Her fluffy brood, snug and safe from harm,
High among the rafters of farmer Dai's old barn.

The tawny and the little owl
Boldly announce with spine-chilling screeches,
Their hungry need for scuttling food;
"Small prey beware!" their eerie cry,
As softer moonlight relieves the eye.

Strange cries are echoing through the night,
As hunters large and small go forth.
The wily fox, the stoat, the rat,
He gruffly barks, they give soprano squeak.
It's nature's way, as food for growing young they seek.

Now tints of light proclaim the dawn,
Each hunter carries back a lifeless kill.
The Great Provider again has satisfied,
As shrill, demanding voices of varying tone,
Greet each proud and laden parent home.

There must be birds in heaven

There must be birds in heaven, no music sweet as theirs,
For sure, they sing like angels, as they wing to heaven our prayers.

The light of day just breaking, from the East across the sky,
It calls the birds to worship, for they know their Lord is nigh.

There must be birds in heaven, as there were that Easter Day;
Two mornings they were silent, when in tomb of stone He lay.

As still as death the silence, 'till tomb was opened wide.
The work of God completed, for no Saviour lay inside.

There must be birds in heaven, 'twas they who saw Him rise;
Pure as they sang in Eden, their notes soared to Paradise.

Now as each dawn approaches, they are called once more to sing.
There must be birds in heaven, giving Glory to our King.
Giving Glory to our King!

This is God's Love

Gentle as a Summer breeze,
Dew-fall at dawning.
Softer than a moonlight beam
Dancing on rippling stream,
This, this is God's Love,
This is God's Love.

Silently we come to Thee,
Spirit of heaven.
Freely flow from God above,
Fill us with Holy Love,
Hear our humble prayer,
Hear our prayer.

Now, the heart is satisfied,
Thirsting no longer.
Grace has touched our simple soul,
With Christ within we're whole.
Thanks be to our God!
Thanks be to God!

Turn again, turn again

There's a balance in nature of air, water, field;
But life form is struggling 'gainst the tide of man's greed.
The skies above cluttered—'tis true and 'tis sad,
Space littered with relics of science 'gone mad'.

How far people travel to harvest the sea,
There's not much room left now, where creatures are free.
Failing to thrive as death stalks at their door,
For greed tolls the bell: "We want more!" "We want more!"

Man just has to find it, naught can be concealed,
The Creature's secrets all brusquely revealed.
So slowly found—so swiftly lost,
Wonders of nature—but oh, at what cost!

Now is the hour, the time and the day,
As this new millennium revolves on its way.
For another millennium, generations to come,
Yes, they'll be the ones left with what we have done!

Turn again, turn again, look hard at earth's plight;
The suffering as millions with nothing take flight.
Turn again, turn again, with compassion and love,
For our God holds the future in His hands above.

The Very First Time

We both wanted it,
We fought in pain, all else forgotten;
Then, waiting dear ones knew, together we cried out,
Mother and child, sharing our triumph,
For the Very First Time.

We walked and talked,
Played and prayed, laughing for sheer delight as years went by.
Mother and child, each new experience ours
For the Very First Time.

Poignant pangs of changing years,
The start of budding womanhood, facing the rugged mountains of life,
Together we climbed as one, Mother and child deepening the bond,
For the Very First Time.

How serene, how calm you were,
Eyes that shone with purest joy, we shared in spirit still my child,
Strong and clear your vows were made,
When heart to heart was given, for the Very First Time.

What happy days of waiting, your dancing eyes had told me all.
Life's seamless circle carries on, together now, your cries rang out,
Mother and child, sharing the triumph for the Very First Time.

We're Ready

The pair of us are eager, real excited you might say,
Might it just be, I wonder, 'cause the family come today?'

We've written lots of letters, we've chatted on the phone,
But somehow, it is nothing quite like talking in our home.

The larder's full and ready, the fridge as well complete,
They're the ones we want to see, the ones we long to greet.

Outside the sun is shining, we spoke to it today,
With very strict instructions not to hide himself away.

I hope they're coming well prepared for fun on land and sea,
Ready to enjoy themselves as a happy family.

Seven days, a week in all, how swiftly time will fly.
"Make the most of it," we say, time enough to say "Goodbye".

'Wings of White'

Ocean spray and salty air,
The throb of angry wind and sea.
Though wild the wind and high the wave,
We find You here, our God.
Refrain:
Then rise my spirit on wings of white,
As seabird soaring, take your flight.
Sing out with joy—unbounded joy,
O'er land and sea, fly home.

Pools of light on sandy shore,
Once more the ocean softly sings.
With healing balm her music flows,
In peace, we find You God.
Refrain:
Then rise my spirit on wings of white,
As seabird soaring, take your flight.
Sing out with joy—unbounded joy,
O'er land and sea, fly home.

A crystal sea before us lies,
On every shore Your praise is heard,
As heavenly choirs full-throated sing,
"Glory to You, our God!"
Refrain:
Then rise my spirit on wings of white,
As seabird soaring, take your flight.
Sing out with joy—unbounded joy,
O'er land and sea, fly home.

Praise

A Thankful Heart

A thankful heart is ever near to God,
Whose Grace and Mercy never cease.
Along this path of thankfulness
God meets us with His Perfect Peace.

A thankful heart that turns to God in prayer,
Sweet gifts of Peace, Hope, Joy will find.
Freely given by His loving hand,
His Sacred Pledge to all mankind.

Oh, grant us thankful hearts, dear Lord;
The Greatest Gift of all he gave.
Christ His One and Only sacrificed,
God's Dearest One our souls to save.

Come now to worship God

Come now to worship God in this His holy place;
We come with joyful hearts and gladly bring to Him our praise.
Before Your throne we bow, Creator, Father God,
Whose Breath gives life to every living creature by His Word.

Each seed lies hidden deep, unseen by human eye,
Until the tender shoots break forth again toward the sky.
How can this come to be? Mankind may never know,
For only God, the Living God has power to make life grow.

Praise our Creator's Love in giving all things good.
Thank Him for gifts of earth, and thank Him for His Holy Word.
Glory to God on high, honour to Christ His Son;
Praise and thanksgiving to His Spirit for all God has done.

Creator God, we praise You

The sun by day, the moon by night,
Stars that guide men by their light.
In these, God's handiwork we see,
Creator God, we praise You.

The winds that blow, the rains that fall,
Life and strength He gives to all.
For God alone controls their power.
Creator God, we praise You.

Harsh rugged creatures of the wild,
Beast of field and stall so mild.
For minds to understand their need,
Creator God, we praise You.

Almighty God, who moves with Love,
Whose blessing flow from heaven above;
O hear our thankful prayers today,
Creator God, we praise You.

Eternal Love

The Lord has done good things for me;
Too great for words to tell.
His Spirit wakes me from my sleep,
He tells me, "All is well".
Praise God for His Eternal Love!

These words bring joy within my heart,
My spirit lifted high.
Protected from the evil one,
Safe Lord, when You are nigh.
Praise God for His Eternal Love!

Your Spirit leads me to Your Word,
My hunger to assuage;
The more I read, the more I learn,
To see You on each page.
Praise God for His Eternal Love!

"Oh, Living Lord, please walk with me,
Help me to share Your Love.
By gentle word and kindly deed,
Until we meet above.
Praise God for His Eternal Love!

Flame of Love

Light of heaven, You walked this earth,
Through You God's Love was shown.
How powerful, how bright the flame,
That drew to You, Your own.

The deepest darkness of our sin,
Drew close around You, closer still;
With anguished cry, Your Light went out.
Completed now, Your Father's Will.

That brightest morn, how clear You shone.
Your Light re-kindled, Living Vine.
Oh, light in us Your Flame of Love,
Until our spirits glow like Thine.

Follow your heart

Follow your heart, it knows the way
To where true Love begins.
Follow your heart, trust in the One
Who hold it 'neath His wings.

Follow your heart, don't be afraid,
Though choices hard arise.
Follow your heart, He understands,
Trust Him, the Ever-Wise.

Follow your heart, your whole life long;
You shall not walk alone.
Follow your heart, His Light shines there,
Until He calls you—HOME.

He understands

Have you ever felt bewildered,
Crying, "Which way do I turn?"
Have you struggled deep within,
As your nerve ends start to burn?

Do you try to go to sleep,
Questions buzzing round your mind?
Bleary-eyed, you leave your bed
Saying, "Life today is one long grind?"

Do you fret at little things,
Wishing you could run and hide?
Years ago, when you were young,
Then, you'd take them 'in your stride'.

How you want to let it out,
Just to TALK to one who cares;
There is a FRIEND who understands,
He'll share the needs of all your prayers.

Faith is such a 'quiet hope',
Trusting that His Word is true.
'Tis in your heart you'll hear Him,
Softly whisp'ring, "I love you!"

His Unfailing Promises

After darkness—
'Light'
After storm—
'Calm'
After restlessness—
'Stillness'
After pain—
'Healing'
After blindness—
'Sight'
After tongue-tied—
'Utterance'
After deafness—
'Hearing'
After silence—
'Speech'
After lameness—
'A dance of joy'
After hunger—
'Feeding'
After thirst—
'Beautiful quenching'
After yearning—
'Meeting'
After sin—
'Forgiveness'
After death—
'LIFE EVERLASTING'.

"I Love You Child"

"I love you child," our Father tells us;
"No need to struggle, no need to fear".
Just be yourself, let Him direct you,
To Him, your path of life is clear.

"I love you child," our Father tells us;
"With Love that grows each time you pray.
Call me often, I will hear you,
I never sleep by night or day."

"I love you child", our Father tells us;
Our Jesus is 'The Way' back home.
Trust and believe, He will not fail you,
God will never leave you all alone.

"I love you child," our Father tells us;
"Be not afraid though eyes grow dim.
My Promise stands, I shall NOT fail you."
He'll gently lead you home to Him.

Rejoice in the Light

Rejoice in the Light that God has given you,
Rejoice in His Light always.
Rejoice in the Light that Christ is offering you,
Rejoice in Him each day.

Rejoice in the Light when dark clouds cover you,
Rejoice when the day is long.
Rejoice in the Light that Christ is offering you,
Rejoice in Him with song.

Rejoice in the Light, go serve the Holy One,
Rejoice though the task be long.
Rejoice in the Light that Christ is offering you,
Rejoice let faith be strong.

Rejoice in the Light, tell others of your hope,
Rejoice in the Saviour Son.
Rejoice in the Light that Christ is offering you,
'Till heaven and earth are one.

Sing

Sing, when your heart is aching,
For music is a wordless prayer.
Bring the deepest pain within you,
God understands, dear one,
Just SING.

Sing, when new joys awake you,
For music gives itself in praise.
Bring your thankful heart before Him,
God understands, dear One,
Just SING.

Sing, when the Spirit moves you,
For music takes us nearer heaven.
Bring your day with all that happens,
God understands, dear one,
Just SING.

Walking with Jesus

Let not your heart be troubled, do not worry at your load,
The Lord our God will surely help you walk along the road.
Refrain:
So praise the Lord with thankful heart,
Assured His Promise stands-
"My child, I'll never leave you,
Just hold fast to my hands."

At each new days awakening, tell the Lord what lies in store.
Trust Him to guide you onward, for He knows what is before.
Refrain:
So praise the Lord with thankful heart,
Assured His Promise stands-
"My child, I'll never leave you,
Just hold fast to my hands."

Be still when worries threaten, offer up a whispered prayer.
Remember He is waiting, rest assured He's always there.
Refrain:
So praise the Lord with thankful heart,
Assured His Promise stands-
"My child, I'll never leave you,
Just hold fast to my hands."

Turn bitterness to sweetness, as Christ would have you do.
To be for Him a messenger, let His Light shine brightly through.
Refrain:
So praise the Lord with thankful heart,
Assured His Promise stands-
"My child, I'll never leave you,
Just hold fast to my hands."

We Are His Own!

Jesus our Saviour, You are all we need;
Friend true and faithful, You have set our hearts free.
We are His own! We are His own!
He shall sustain us, we are His own!

Jesus our Saviour, You know all our care;
We put our trust in You, knowing that You are there.
We are His own! We are His own!
He shall sustain us, we are His own!

Jesus our Saviour, You rose to live once more,
Opened our way to heaven, our Living Hope ever sure.
We are His own! We are His own!
He shall sustain us, we are His own!

Jesus is Lord of all, let our voices blend,
Our Rock of Certainty till our life here shall end.
We are His own! We are His own!
He shall sustain us, we are His own!

We're on the way to heaven

We're on the way to heaven,
by Grace and Grace alone.
For there our Saviour waits for us,
He waits to take us home.

We're on the way to heaven,
The winding road is long.
But Jesus cheers our every step,
He teaches us His song.

We're on the way to heaven,
Where dear ones stand and wait.
Our Jesus stands with open arms,
He'll open wide the gate.

We're on the way to heaven,
Come, join us on the way.
Tell Jesus you will follow Him
More closely every day.

We're on the way to heaven,
We're only passing through.
By faith in Christ who leads the way.
Praise God, His Word is true.

For the Little Ones

A Bushy Tale

Two twinkling eyes were watching me,
Head set saucily askew.
I could almost hear him say,
"Whatever are you going to do?"

Quite unperturbed I carried on,
The task was skill-demanding;
Fumbling fingers, blue with cold,
Like castanets my teeth were chattering.

It had taken weeks of planning,
To create this great surprise.
Miles of ropes and shaky ladder;
Can't keep away those twinkling eyes.

The intricate design was done,
Ladders, pipes and swinging ropes;
Highway to a nutty prize,
Triumphant outcome of my hopes.

My home no longer silent wakes,
Children singing, voices shrill.
With fingers crossed, we wait to see
My clever squirrel show his skill.

A Poem For Ted

"Where is my Ted? Oh, where is my Ted?
He sorts out all my muddle;
How CAN you make me go to bed
Without my friend to cuddle?"

"What colour is your Ted?" they ask;
"How quickly they forget.
If he could purr or wag his tail,
He'd be the family PET!"

"I don't know when his Birthday was,
Like mine, it can't be long.
But I can tell him everything,
He never say's I'm wrong!"

Removal men arrived today,
With boxes everywhere.
They asked me, "Have you lost your Ted?
Go, look in Gran's armchair!"

Mum whispered, "Have you got your Ted?"
Then kissed us both goodnight;
I waved my hand, he waved his paw.
"I love you Ted, sleep tight!"

Billy Bee

Young Bill is a humble bumble bee,
Surprisingly quite gentle.
He stops to look at pretty flowers,
He's rather sentimental.

We know that bees are busy chaps,
Buzzing loudly all the day.
Have you ever stopped to wonder
Why they should behave that way?

Our Bill is very keen to learn
What busy bees should do.
"Come shopping Bill," his mother said,
"and fill you baskets like I do."

Young Bill was feeling rather tired,
Baskets full to the brim.
"Well done young Bill!" His mother hums,
She really was quite proud of him.

If you should meet our busy Bill,
Please don't disturb, just watch him strive
To fill those baskets on his knees,
With sweetest pollen for the hive.

The Crab

A curious creature is the crab,
Hiding in odd places.
Some are small, some very large,
With pokey little faces.

Down in the sand, beneath the rocks
He scuttles into holes.
Take care now—as you seek him,
His claws can nip small toes!

"Let's catch a crab," the children cry,
With bent pin and a line.
But pleading eyes that watch you
Get put back, every time.

Some crabs have homes, and some do not,
Depends on who they be.
Some like to keep on moving
Or, 'rent-a-home', like me.

Remember, when you meet a crab
To always be polite.
Hungry ones look pretty cool,
Beware! They all can BITE!

Discovering Colours

Colours have a lesson
For those who wish to see.
Nature's palette, made by God,
A kaleidoscope for me.

Come, let us look at colours,
Discover what they tell.
God uses colours in His world,
His creatures know this well.

A thousand blues, a million greens,
Has anybody counted?
Shades of Autumn, tints of Spring,
A glorious picture mounted.

What colour guides the honey bee
To where the nectar flows?
What colours warn our lovely birds
Of poisonous ants or toads?

God, in His wisdom, paints the coats
Of creatures where they roam.
A wondrous blend of patterns rare
Protect them in their home.

Mankind inspired paints all he sees
Of green, of red, of blue.
So hard to choose, too hard to say,
"I love them all—don't you?"

Guess My Name

I'm a jolly little fellow
With a big, round tummy.
All boys and girls love me
Why? Because I am YUMMY!

You may find me in boxes,
Or up high on a shelf.
You may even find me
Hiding, all by myself.

Chicken eggs can be eaten
Out of pan, or out of pot.
Please—don't try to boil me,
I will melt when I am HOT!

Have you guessed who I am yet
Wrapped up prettily or plain?
Of course you've got the answer:
'EASTER EGG' is my real name!

Ivor the Spider

Ivor the spider is a very odd fellow,
With long hairy legs, and big spots of yellow.
Young insects and flies, beware—be polite,
For if Ivor is hungry, he may fancy a BITE!

He's a shy little person, preferring the dark
Of holes in brick walls, or trees in the park.
With eight wriggly legs, and eyes on his head,
He's not the 'best friend' to find in your BED!

When Sports Day comes round Ivor's 'Top of the Pops',
With matching trainers, and four pairs of socks.
Running and Long Jump, he wins them by far,
Then in the Obstacle, why Ivor's the STAR!

Internet, Megga-Bite leave him confused,
But when we say "Web Site", Ivor's amused.
If in a cupboard you meet with a spider,
Don't be afraid, it just might be IVOR!

Little Betty Butterfly

On a warm Summer day,
Little Betty would play
'Hide and Seek' between the flowers.

She was pretty and bright
As she fluttered in flight,
And danced with her friends for hours.

In fields mauve with clover,
The butterflies hover,
These flowers are full of good things.

For clover holds nectar
To feed and sustain her,
While the sunshine warms her wings.

"Who made you dear Betty,
So bright and so pretty?"
"God made me," Betty replies.

The Little Owl

The little owl is really small,
Very like my teddy bear.
Yes, he can turn his head right round,
And he watches everywhere.

At sunset, when the sun goes down,
The little owl starts blinking.
Then stretch and shake his feathers brown,
Oh look! I think he's winking.

The black crows caw and white gulls cry,
A cheeky robin singing.
As silent as a puff of wind,
The little owl goes winging.

Unseen, unheard, the owl will search
For baby mouse or sparrow.
The owl's sharp ears hear every sound,
Claws striking swift as arrow.

Beware, take care, dear little mouse,
There is danger overhead.
Stay safe 'neath hedge and grasses tall,
As you scuttle home to bed.

Squeak

I saw a little mouse one day,
It ran across my path.
He wasn't very big you know,
But how he made me laugh!

With shiny tail and furry skin,
His feet all small and pink;
He stopped awhile to look at me,
I'm sure I saw him wink!

He scuttled here, he scuttled there,
I had to wait and see
If he was playing "Hide and Seek",
Or simply teasing me.

Out from a crack he brought a nut,
It was a great surprise!
Then, he sat down and nibbled it
Right there, before my eyes!

He turned around and flicked his tail,
The message was quite plain.
Who knows, if I keep careful watch,
I may see him again.

If you should hear a rustling sound
Beneath your stony wall,
It just might be our mousey friend,
So quick, so bright, so small.

A Taste of Christmas

Be Glad

Good shepherds way out on the hills,
Be glad, be glad, be glad:
Such wondrous news the angels tell,
Be glad, be glad, be glad.

Way high above, the glowing star
resting, resting, resting.
For now her journey is complete,
Resting, resting, resting.

Sweet Mother of the Holy Child,
Cry out, cry out, cry out.
This day you bring to birth God's Son,
Cry out, cry out, cry out.

In holy awe she greets her King,
"Jesus, Lord, Messiah!"
Her Holy Babe smiles in His sleep,
Jesus, Lord, Messiah.

The latch is lifting, shepherds come,
Behold, behold, behold.
Silent and humble they adore,
Behold, behold, behold.

Then come the Wise and Holy three,
With awe, with awe, with awe.
Present their Gifts on bended knee,
With awe, with awe, with awe.

God's humble ones were first to know,
Blessing, blessing, blessing.
So shall it be before God's throne,
Blessing, blessing, blessing.

With holy angels we shall sing,
"Glory, Hallelujah!"
Sing, "Welcome to our Saviour King!
Glory, Hallelujah!"

Christmas Blessings One and All

A blessed Christmas one and all,
That flows with Joy and Love.
It was upon that Christmas Morn,
God's Gift came from above.

Look up and see the Morning Star,
That shines before the dawn.
So did that Star of Bethlehem,
Reveal where Christ was born.

Oh hear within your hearts the call,
That thrills the very soul.
And pray for those with broken hearts,
Christ came to make them whole.

A blessed Christmas one and all,
His Star has shed its Light.
As we enjoy the Festive Day,
That follows Holy Night.

Noel, Noel, Oh Son of God

So long ago on grassy hill, the shepherds heard this song,
"Your Saviour King is born today",
Thus sang the heavenly throng.
With hasty breath and running feet,
They hurried down to see—
The King of kings, a tiny Babe, so small, so frail was He.

They knew the Promise was fulfilled,
"Messiah, Lord", their cry;
How could they know? How could they tell
Their King was sent to die?
They brought their gift, a tiny lamb in quiet humility,
And there among the lowly beasts, worshipped the King to be.

From far-off lands the Wise Men came,
Responding to the 'Sign',
And bending low on weary knee, they worshipped The Divine.
Gold, frankincense and myrrh they brought
As gifts before the stall.
Symbolic off'rings for His life, to Christ the Lord of all.

Two thousand years have now gone past
Since these events occurred.
The faultless life and death of Christ
We find within God's Word.
With grateful minds, and loving hearts we worship here today,
The Babe, the Man, the Son of God still beckons from the hay.

We bow our heads to worship You, O risen, glorious King!
The gift You treasure most of all,
Dear Lord, our hearts we bring.
Noel, Noel, O Son of God, Noel this Christmas morn,
With all the hosts of heav'n we join-
"Praise God, His Son is born!"

Listen to the Echo

Listen to the echo, as it rolls around the world,
Like wavelengths from a mobile phone,
The sound may still be heard.
Listen to the echo vibrate across the years,
The shepherds stunned to silence, as glory filled their ears.

Listen to the echo, a faint and distant cry;
Creator of the universe, soothed by lullaby.
Listen to the echo, as faithful shepherds come,
Believing hearts and simple faith, their offering to God's Son.

Listen to the echo, with joy the weary three
Brought frankincense and gold and myrrh,
Messiah, Lord to Thee.
Listen to the echo, amid the rowdy throng,
Son of God, our Saviour, gave His blood for mankind's wrong.

Listen to the echo, Christ's Day draws ever near;
For those who own Christ as God's Son,
Hell's terrors hold no fear.
Listen to the echo, that mighty trumpet blast;
No place to hide, nowhere to run,
He'll call His OWN—at last!

Pause a Moment

Amidst the jingle and the jangle,
Sparkling lights and children's toys;

Amidst the hustle and the bustle,
Laughter light from girls and boys;

Amidst the meeting and the greeting,
Parcels bright that please the eye;

Pause a moment—'midst the singing,
Sense a joy too deep for speaking,

DID YOU HEAR HEAVEN'S BABY CRY?

What a Gift

What a Gift this is indeed,
The greatest Gift of all.
So simply wrapped in swaddling cloths,
And laid to sleep in draughty stall.

What a Gift this is indeed,
Believing hearts beat fast with joy.
With love and awe we welcome Him,
God's Gift of Grace, God's Holy Boy.

What a glorious Gift indeed,
So freely given with selfless Love;
Born helpless Babe, as helpless man he died-
To rise our Saviour, Christ above.

SDG   Marjorie Wheeler

The Shy Little Star

(Children's' Story)

The Shy Little Star

This is a story about a very, very small star, who was so SHY, so FRIGHTENED, she would hide behind the clouds.

A strange thing happened to the little star one night, would you like to know what happened?

She had a visitor, an ANGEL sent from God with a SPECIAL JOB for her to do.

As the angel whispered to the tiny star, she began to feel all warm inside. The more the angel told her, the more she glowed, because it was such a WONDERFUL message.

As she listened, this little star grew BIGGER and BIGGER, she felt so HAPPY, and was shining so much that everyone down below could see her now.

Far, far away in the East, there were three CLEVER men, who studied the stars. They watched the stars, and a bit like our weather today, could tell what was going to happen. They too saw our shining star, and they knew that her message was about a King coming to the world.

This STAR IN THE EAST was a sign to them that a Holy Child had been born—do you know His name?
Of course, it was JESUS, THE HOLY SON OF GOD.

The star began to move, so these THREE WISE MEN followed her with presents for this King that was coming.
They took three gifts, these were GOLD; FRANKINCENSE; and MYRRH, each one had a special meaning

The angel had told the star where to stop, so this she did, giving a lovely light into the stable where Mary was rocking her Baby in a manger cradle.

Soon, there were SHEPHERDS at the door, and we KNOW they had heard the ANGEL MESSENGER out in the fields where they were keeping the sheep and lambs safe.

These shepherds were the VERY FIRST people to hear that God's Holy Baby Son had been born. They were told just where to find the BABY— now what did those angels say? "IN A MANGER IN BETHLEHEM," and this was EXACTLY where they found MARY, JOSEPH and the BABY JESUS.

Do you remember the little shepherd boy who brought a tiny baby lamb for Jesus? The shepherds all knelt down before the Baby, they were so sure that He was really the Son of God that He was THE MESSIAH.

Not long after, along came the THREE WISE MEN with their three GIFTS. Can you see in your mind the shepherds who had come in their ROUGH, DARK clothes? Now here were the MAGI (WISE MEN) coming wearing clothes of very bright COLOURS and they were wearing crowns with many JEWELS.

After they had all given the gifts, and knelt to pray for the Baby King, they went away, and it was quiet in the stable while the star shone down with light and warmth.

God could have asked a big comet with a long, long tail to guide the Wise Men, but instead it was our tiny, shy and rather frightened little star that was given such an important job to do.
That tiny, shy star is still known as THE STAR OF BETHLEHEM today.

Marjorie's Snippets

Marjorie's Snippets

Ash

It had been one of the roughest nights of bombing since the dreaded doodle-bugs began to come booming over our streets.

People were used to the screaming of bombs, followed by the ear-shattering explosions, then more and more of the same, until the mind became numbed as time went by. People, shivering as they huddled beneath the city would laugh wildly at preposterously silly jokes.

This night was different. The off-key tone of their planes did not end with the screaming of falling bombs, where the experienced were able to identify almost exactly where this monster had fallen. No, this time, the drone stopped, just as if a tap had been turned off, and there was silence—a grim silence, as people waited with breath held in suspense until it came, the eardrum cracking explosion. Another home GONE!

The scene was indeed grim, everywhere there was dust, thick and dark. The landscape of twisted steel and broken glass, brick walls, looked like a crazy set for a horror film.

It was on such a night, that my friend and I were caught in an air raid of some force. The courageous teams of fire fighters were urging folk to go into the underground shelter, and we were carried along with the tide, as it were. We waited there for the All Clear signal to come.

Once inside the station, when our eyes had adjusted to the eerie light, we could see that all the people around us had the mark of a rough cross on their foreheads. The firemen explained that the markings were to show that those people needed to be taken to 'a place of safety', where they would be gently cared for.

So too were we marked with a cross. As Christians we had just come out from our weekly Communion Service for Ash Wednesday, so we had the symbol of Christ's Cross on our brow also. I was struck with the thought, that just as those in the shelter were marked to be given shelter and care: so too were we, marked to know the Shelter and Care of our Saviour Lord. This small link is one I shall never forget.

The Best of Friends

Isn't it wonderful to know that you can talk to a true friend about 'anything'. To know that they can be completely trusted, they will never give away the secrets you share.

No matter what you have done, a true friend does not judge you, but wants to help you find the best way forward: indeed, a true friend will always 'be there' for you.

Jesus, actually calls Himself a friend," I am the Friend of Sinners", How comforting that is!

Are you in need of such a friend I wonder? It is so easy: just TELL HIM—He's always waiting!

The Blackbird

I have a friend who has a gift for caring for injured, or orphaned baby birds. Mary tends these helpless ones with immense tenderness and wisdom. All this care allows the young ones to thrive, and they grow into fine specimens of sparrow, swallow, blue tit or blackbird even. When she is quite sure they are ready, the little ones are taken back to where they were found. Makes me think, are we not told that our Father knows even when the tiniest sparrow falls. How pleased He must be to see Mary working so carefully to save His birds.

One evening, Mary brought a small bird to show me, and what a joy it was to hold such a minute warm bundle, and feed it by hand with tiny meal worms. The other evening, Mary brought a very young blackbird to show me, this delicate creature sat completely calm in her hands. I was surprised to see that he had a mottled breast, not unlike that of a thrush, I would have said it was a thrush had she asked me.

As I watched it, she placed the bird on her fore arm, it was enchanting to watch him slowly cutch down on her arm, meanwhile making the most gentle of tweets, so musical and sweet. Slowly, so slowly, his tiny eyes closed, and he was asleep there on her arm.

Later, she gently passed him to me, and having scrutinised me with his bright black eyes, he made the same lovely musical notes, and to my delight, settled down on my arm too.

As I watched Mary so lovingly enfolding this beautiful bird between her hands, softly caressing the tiny head, until, feeling safe and comforted he was lulled to sleep by the sheer love of his rescuer.

Is it not a comforting thought, that when we ourselves turn to sleep in the arms of our own Wonderful Rescuer, we too will feel safe and comforted in His tender Love for us!

The Calm of Gentle Breathing

We begin breathing with our first gasp of surprise at the strange new world of new birth, gently ending with the quiet last breath at the moment of death. When we say the Name 'Jesus', it can flow within our breathing, first the "Je----Sus." Saying this in a quiet way can become a form of prayer.

So many people seem to live on a sort of 'super over drive', and many do find themselves in hospital with varying problems. They are in danger of getting out of control.

There is a way to slow down, to step aside from our many daily pressures. We may, as Christians find that our heartbeat does slow down as we pray, calming our agitation.

One does not have to use the word Jesus, indeed, any word associated with love or beauty will have the same lovely effect. It may take a little practise to find the key that suits you individually, but the outcome will be the same. Those over-strung nerves will slowly be eased and a few precious moments of calm within does works wonders.

Do try—I learnt from a friend, and so hope you may also learn from my simple words.

The Dawn Chorus

I am sure many of us wake up very early sometimes, just lately, this has become the norm. for me. I open my curtains and see the first hint of light in the East, a lovely sight, until that thin line of light widens from the East, all is perfect silence.

Then comes just one crystal clear note, piercing the air. There is a pause, then another crystal clear note echoes it. I lean out as far as I dare to catch that distant, so sweet echo, and just have to thank God that my ageing ears have been able to hear that First Birdsong at Dawn.

Within moments, our tiny soloist has been joined by a full-throated feathered Choir. An expert would be able to identify each singer by their notes, what a wonderful gift that is for sure.

How delighted our Keeper of the Sparrow must be to know that each day His birds praise Him in beautiful feathered song!

Kindly Shepherd

I used to be able to look out of my window at a small green paddock. At this time of the year, there would be a small flock of sheep calmly browsing there. It had become a daily ritual for many of us living close by to count the sheep, to check whether any were missing.

Should one or two be missing, we knew that they would be snug in the barn with their new-born lambs beside them, or waiting quietly for their time to come.

The owner of the paddock is a retired farmer, and this small flock are his sheep. It was a lovely picture watching this shepherd as he moved among them. He would walk down the field every day, and the sheep would come up to him. This gentle shepherd would talk to them quietly, even place his hand on a head or two as he did so. As soon as the gate opened the eager flock rushed up the field to greet him with lots of soft bleating. I shall never forget the sight and sound of all this, even now, it still touches my heart.

Does this not remind us of the One Good Shepherd, who may just as gently draw near to us, and just as softly speak in our hearts, whilst comforting or encouraging as we need.

Yr Arglwydd yw fy Mugail da—The Lord is my Shepherd indeed.

Light

I was looking up a quotation in my husband's Concordance one day, and such a simple thing happened, yet it made a great impression on me. Allow me to share it with you dear reader.

I found what I was seeking quite easily, and began to put the coloured ribbons into place, so that I might find the words easily next time they were needed.

This one ribbon looked was a rather dull dark green nothing more. But, as I lifted it up to put between the pages, I was suddenly most surprised to find it was glowing brightly as the light caught it. What had once looked so dark and uninteresting, was now a beautiful glowing ribbon.

It was such a simple surprise, but how amazingly it became a blessing to me, bringing the simple message to my heart, that when we stand in the Light of Christ, we too shall glow beautifully as did that dull green ribbon. Praise God!

Love

Some years ago, we had a large garden and our neighbour's garden lay across the far end, there was always kindly advice coming to us newcomers across the garden fence.

An elderly gentleman who lived there was a very keen gardener, and his garden was always so neat and tidy, with plenty of wonderful plants and vegetables all coming in their due season. His seeds were carefully planted each year at a set time, such as Michaelmas Day, or Easter.

One day, I was happily cutting a lovely bunch of sweet peas and thinking to myself how wonderful their colours were, and what a marvellous palette our God uses to paint them, as one does, I muttered to myself how it was a pity to cut too many, thinking that was all I would have. Just then, our neighbour spoke to me.

"Them sweet peas of yours are far from over me dear, the more you cut and give away, the more will grow in their place.

He was absolutely right you know. Within a few days, the bush was bursting with beautiful colours once again, all ready to give away as 'cheer-you-up' bunches.

Later on in the year, we had a bumper crop of green beans, 'runner beans' I think they were called. We were more than happy to share these with others who had no vegetable garden, and pretty soon, there were pots of runners merrily boiling right across our estate.

Our kindly neighbour spoke to me again, and told me, "The more you take of those there beans, the more will come in their place." He was absolutely right again!

One quiet afternoon, quietly sitting relaxed in the garden, I could see how this thought could apply to 'love', for surely, the more we give our love away, all the more bountifully will our heavenly Father replenish our hearts with His LOVE.

The Old Garden Shed

You may be rather surprised to find I am writing about an old garden shed today, especially as I no longer have one, but it might be helpful to take a look inside this old shed, we may learn something.

Years ago, when there was a shed in my life, it doubled as a bike shed, so many did of course in those days. I suppose one might call it a 'Put anything you like in it' type of shed. You may well have one even now. I would imagine your shed to be lovely and neat, with tidy places to hang all the tools, and those tools being clean, bright and shiny each and every one 'Ready for Action!'

I am ashamed to say mine was nothing like that. It was so full, I could hardly get through the door, full of higgledy-piggledy of the oddest things. Old bike parts, and old broken pram, (ah, happy days!) a spade, a hoe here and there and "Ouch!" an old garden fork, and scraggy strings of very dead onions, need I go on? There was a smell in there, kind of comforting in an odd way, musty, warm and full of aromas long forgotten.

Let's take another look at those tools, take them out into the bright sunshine then—oh my! That was quite a shock! They are rusty, and have huge clods of dried earth clinging to them, some are even worse, bent or broken. Did someone whisper "You should be ashamed" Quite right too, oh, so TRUE!

Maybe our hearts are sometimes like that old shed, perhaps we should take a look once in a while. "No-one" Paul tells us, "is perfectly clean, none of us completely free from clogging sin, only Jesus is the Perfect One." We need the Gardener of our Hearts to Spring Clean for us, only He can refurbish us—our personal shed will then be 'Clean and Ready for His use!"

One in spirit by Grace

This little item is written for all whose hearts are united within a Chain of Prayer. The words are simple, but do carry a significant meaning for each of us when we unite in spirit, praying in love for the 'needs of others'.

One evening, I was preparing to go out and decided to put on a pretty necklace, as I looked at the string of gems, these thoughts came to mind, so I wrote them down to share with others.

The gems on every necklace need to be held in place by some form of THREAD, this has to be strong and enduring. The thread in our Prayer Necklace must surely be a THREAD of LOVE, from the caring of our hearts.

The jewels that make up the necklace are the most precious part, and I saw these as being THOSE WHO HAVE NEED of our prayers: most certainly, none should be lost!

Every necklace needs a good CLASP to complete the circle. This of course, carries the vital task of holding the COMPLETE necklace together. Most surely, the CLASP to our necklace of prayer has to JESUS HIMSELF. He will never weaken, nor give way. He holds fast within the Circle of Love all the COMPASSION that flows from our hearts, which He carries to our Heavenly Father.

To be part of such a necklace is a tremendous privilege. It becomes ever more amazing as we realize that as these chains are used, the prayers become like pebbles in a pond, forever moving outwards and at the same time over lapping one with the other. Makes one think of that lovely hymn that says:

"As o'er each continent and island the dawn leads on another day,

The voice of prayer is never silent, nor dies the strain of praise away."

Pure Water

I had a shower this morning, nothing unusual in that you must be thinking. A thought came to my mind as enjoyed the comforting warm and generous crystal clear flow about me.

How safe we feel beneath such water, no danger for us is there, but for many in this world water can be the most dangerous part of their daily life. For them, there is no clear streaming fountain, just a rusty pail of dirty, clouded, often foul-smelling liquid, wherein lurk untold numbers of life-threatening germs.

We just turn on a tap, without thinking, and out comes an instant and plentiful supply. For so many suffering people are obliged to use their sparse supply of unwholesome fluid, not merely for washing, but for cooking, drinking and yes—for FEEDING their babies!

When we swallow a glass of water, do we swallow a toxic potion? No, most surely we do NOT! I would ask the question . . . . "WHY SHOULD THEY?"

Our Creator gave us all pure water upon the earth, it is we, mankind who have polluted it, by sending out vast quantities of industrial waste, and disturbing natural drainage areas, by deforestation and such.

Maybe some readers will remember that amazing project, 'Feed the World', this has broadened now to include the need for 'Water for the World', and tremendous work is being done by many Charities such as Tear Fund, Save the Children and such, by providing deep wells which give the needy ones PURE WATER. As we pass a glass of our pure water to our children, maybe we should spare a thought for helpless little ones with only dirty water to drink.

St. Kevin and the bird

Saint Kevin was deep in prayer beneath the trees. A small bird settled on Saint Kevin's open hand as the good saint was so still, that she built a nest in the palm of his hand, and laid her eggs there.

The gentle saint loved the little bird so much, he would not remove her, but kept his hand open all the time, until the little eggs hatched, the wee birds grew feathers, and eventually left this unusual nest.

Is it not a beautiful picture. It brought to my mind the words of one of my favourite hymns which says this—'and I will trust in You alone.' A simple but lovely lesson this, thinking of the complete trust that tiny bird put in Saint Kevin, is this not the same trust we should have in our heavenly Father?

Such a lovely thought

Just close your eyes for a moment, and imagine a scene when you felt so much love, that you knew you had to be extra gentle with that person, or delicate thing even, like holding someone who is very dear, very precious to you, such as holding a new-born baby for the first time, what an amazing miracle that is to be sure. One of those times when there is no need for words, that feeling of deep love flowing between heart and heart with a loved one. I am sure that you will have many tender memories of you own.

The next time we experience this deep warmth, may it remind us quite simply of: HOW MUCH MORE DOES GOD OUR FATHER TENDERLY LOVE US

Thank You For The Storm

You may well be thinking, 'Has she lost her way' actually saying Thank you for a Storm! Just bear with me a while, we might find there another meaning to that word 'Storm'.

It is quite normal for us at some point in our lives to pass through traumatic storms of life, what people might refer to as "Going through a BAD PATCH!" These are times when we are really hurting, such as following a serious accident; knowing the pain of losing the one person who was your 'rock' in life. There can be mental hurts (storms) as well, these can be so cruel; how easily we fall into temptation's wily way and let depression tighten a grip on us. For sure, there are probably as many as Heinz Variety of such storms.

At such times, when we are blessed with dear friends who are strong in their faith and trust, friends who will quietly 'sit beside us' and simply 'listen'. Through them, the Man who could calm the stormy seas, will CALM OUR STORMS with understanding and Love.

Should someone dear to you be in the throes of one of life's storms, although it may feel rather inadequate not having words to say, just 'holding a hand,' letting your 'caring heart' beat in time with theirs so quietly, it is so true—LOVE IS THE KEY.

As that persistent meerkat would say: "Simples."

That Stitch in Time

A stitch in time saves nine, they say. Of course that is very true. Just pause a moment, stop to think, how could this work for you?

Just consider for a moment how you have been today. Has frustration, fret or trouble discoloured what you say?

Sometimes it does not hurt I've found, to pull oneself up short. To look at 'me' from outside in, this could be a timely thought.

A stitch in time saves nine, 'tis true, but is there more to mend? Could a kindly thought, or gentle word, make me a BETTER FRIEND?

Thoughts on Mountains

How inspiring it can be to be among mighty mountains. I know this only too well, having grown up beneath such grandeur, maybe some of you reading this will nod in agreement, remembering times when you too have sensed their awesome majesty.

It must be wonderful to be able to actually climb right to the mountain top, but sometimes it can be even more awesome to stand before a circle of rugged peaks, and feel the intense depth of their power in one's heart.

I can well understand why compulsive climbers describe their feelings as being 'the call of the mountains', in a similar way I imagine, so to will those who sail the oceans describe how they feel as being 'the call of the sea.'

In the solitude and stillness found beneath these wondrous ranges here in Wales, or anywhere around the world, there is little room for pride or boasting; rather one has a tremendous sense of humility just standing there soaking it all in. Maybe many, like myself, feel compelled to Praise the Creator of such WONDERS!

Quiet Meditations

SILENCE

The storm had passed by, it was the SILENCE that woke me, a beautiful silence, when my thoughts turned to thinking of You, my Lord.

A SILENCE deep within the heart of Mary, the Chosen Mother of God's Son, as she dwelt upon that wondrous message received from the Angel Gabriel.

The SILENCE that followed the travail of Your birth Lord, a profound silence of maidenly bliss blended with the deepest awe, as both Mary and Joseph, for the moment, shared the unspeakable awareness that they were the first people on earth to see, to touch, the Holy Son of God. It is an overwhelming thought, and there was SILENCE, because no human voice could express just how they felt in those exquisite moments.

The SILENCE that suddenly enfolded those breathless excited shepherds as they saw before them the Infant Messiah, exactly as the angelic host had told them. Then they related to Mary and Joseph all the angels had said to them, and in SILENCE, Mary treasured the words in her heart. As life went forward, we are told how Mary pondered these Truths in her heart as she saw them unfolding before her.

There was a stunned SILENCE in the Temple, where gathered the most learned of men to discuss holy matters. They listened, SILENT and amazed, as the young Boy spoke intensely and articulately with such deep knowledge of the Truths of the Scriptures.

The SILENCE of the night, as with stars still above You Lord, You joined in beautiful, prayerful communion with God, Your very own True Father, when hearts and Spirits united as One.

When we too, come in SILENCE to wait upon You dear Lord, we are blessed with such a deep closeness to God, our heavenly Father, as He graciously 'touches our souls.'

How profound and utterly lonely was the SILENCE in that brutal desert throughout those 40 days and nights. When, at Your weakest Lord, in the SILENCE of the 'darkness of evil', You, as the human man, were met by Satan's most cruel wiles of temptations, not once; not twice; but thrice!

No human mind could possibly know the dark forces upon You there, but, Blessed Son of God, the SILENCE was shattered as each threatening temptation was met by Your Victory, not once; not twice, but thrice!.

Then, in the deep exhaustion of soul that followed, God sent His angels to gently, SILENTLY, minister to You, His Beloved One.

Time was short for You, Lord Jesus; days filled with the draining of Spirit as you healed, taught and prepared Your shepherds to follow Your command, and "Feed my sheep".

One can imagine the sounds echoing around that ugly hillside of Golgotha. The screams of the crucified, the harsh shouts of the Roman soldiers, the pitiless hammer, as blow, by blow, by blow, they NAILED You Jesus to Your cross. There were no screams, no cries of agony, the Holy Lamb went to His slaughter in SILENCE!

As they lifted up body and cross, the daytime sky went as black as night: a rippling gasp of horror rolled across the hillside, later, came the storm, the earthquake, and the FINAL WORDS of the FORSAKEN ONE. Then, absolute SILENCE, broken only by the anguished weeping of the Mother of the crucified Christ.

There can be no deeper SILENCE than that of the tomb. We will never know how this was broken, save from the Gospel accounts of Christ's Resurrection Morn, then, and only then, may we break our own shocked, private SILENCE to acclaim with a 'Joy Beyond Bounds'—

"Christ is RISEN!"—He is RISEN indeed!"
!HALELLUJAH!—HALELLUJAH!"—HALELLUJAH!"
Amen, Amen, Amen

The DARKEST Day

The fairest face we'll ever know
Was battered, scarred and torn;
Black and blue from hefty blow,
And pierced by cruellest thorn.

The torso whipped and torn apart,
Again—again—again.
The mocking and the chafing chains,
All this, from mortal men!

God's ordained Will was carried out
As Pilot's hands were wet.
The frenzied crowds roared, "Crucify!"
God's Sacrifice was set.

Upon His back with brutal hands
Jarred down the crudest cross;
Up to the 'Hill of Death' He swayed,
Our gain, His bitterest loss.

Hearts were breaking, tears flowed down,
As many moaned to see:
A gentle cloth to wipe His brow,
A man to share His agony.

As nails split sinew, nerve and bone,
"Father, forgive," His cry.
As Moses lifted snake and staff,
God's Son was raised to die.

Our mortal sins on Sacred Flesh
Were laid that darkest day.
As Father-less, He tasted Hell-
The utmost price to pay!

They sorrowed deeply, wept and prayed,
His faithful flock forlorn.

But we, praise God, see empty tomb,
And bless that 'RISEN MORN!'
And bless that 'RISEN MORN!'

His Stars

How brightly shone those orbs of light
Against the blackness of the night.
Those stars, He named them one by one,
The Holy Word, God's only Son.

The angel Choirs announced with joy
The earthly birth of heaven's Boy.
A myriad stars heard what they said,
One Star alone, watched o'er His bed.

He knelt and prayed with anguished cries,
His stars gazed down with helpless eyes.
Muffled footsteps, flick'ring lights,
One kiss that sealed His fate that night.

No stars to watch His agony,
Those stumbling steps to Calvary.
Crude nails, persistent hammer's blow,
Near death—His Father let Him go.

The Morning Star before the day
Watched as the stone was rolled away.
'Midst rainbow hues He walks once more,
The Crucified—now RISEN!
The Crucified—now RISEN!

Lightning Source UK Ltd.
Milton Keynes UK
UKOW04f0044060214

225946UK00002B/24/P